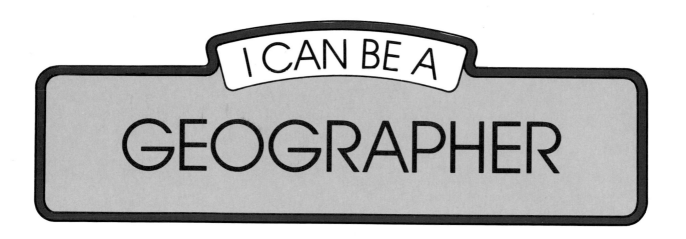

I CAN BE A
GEOGRAPHER

By Paul P. Sipiera

CHILDRENS PRESS®
CHICAGO

Library of Congress Cataloging-in-Publication Data

Sipiera, Paul P.
  I can be a geographer / by Paul P. Sipiera.
      p.   cm.
  Summary: Discusses the different subjects
geographers must know and the various jobs they can
perform.
  ISBN 0-516-01961-9
  1.   Geography—Vocational guidance—Juvenile
literature. [1. Geographers. 2. Occupations.]
I.   Title.
G65.S57   1990
910'.23—dc20

90-2198
CIP
AC

Dedicated to Douglas L. Hicks, a good
friend and geographer

PICTURE DICTIONARY

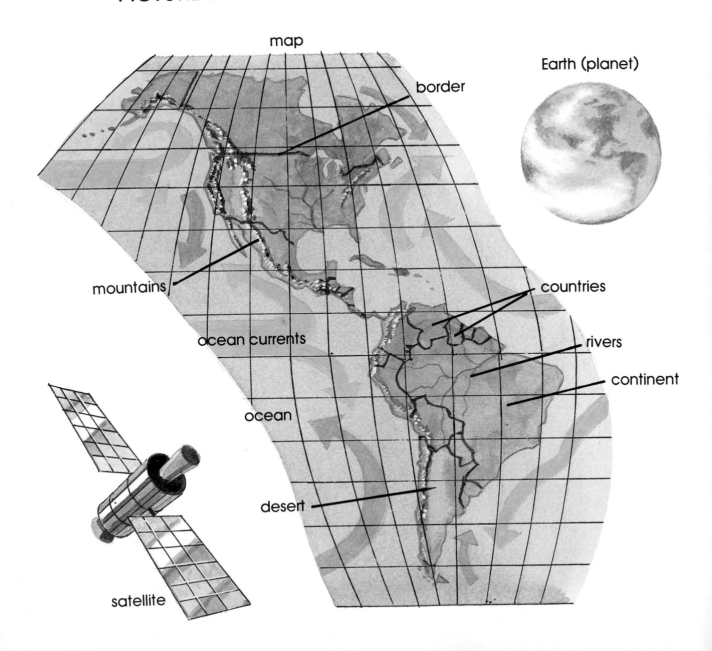

oil

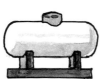
natural gas

coal

Natural resources

(soil) erosion—wasteland

plants

animals

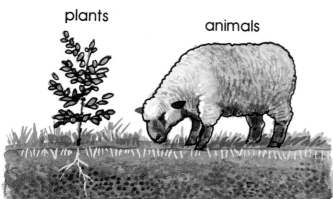
soil

weather

climate

geographer

field study

rain forest

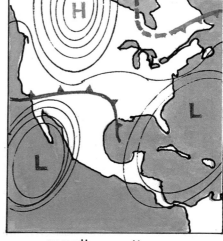
weather patterns

population

Shepherds (above left) move sheep along the east end of Lake Titicaca in Bolivia. A goat herd (above right) near Bouza in Niger. The force of the waves (below) has carved arches into the soft siltstone found along the coast of New Zealand's North Island.

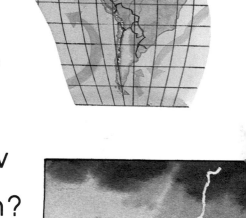

What do you know about the place where you live? Are there mountains nearby? How far is it from the ocean?

weather

What is the weather like? What are the people like? Questions like these are answered by people called geographers— people who study geography.

geographer

A globe is shaped like the earth. This globe is turned to the continent of North America. Can you find Canada, Florida, and Cuba on this globe? Can you see the Rocky Mountains that run from north to south?

Geography is the study of places. A geographer can tell us about different places and the people who live there. To better understand the world we live in, we need to know geography.

6

Geographers study ice-covered mountains and tropical islands in the South Pacific in order to find out how they are formed.

Geographers study the earth. They examine the shape of continents and the location of mountains. Deserts, oceans, and rivers are important to the

Earth (planet)

7

geographer. From their studies, geographers make maps of our world.

Maps tell us about the earth's surface. Some maps show us the boundaries of countries. Some maps show us the location of cities and roads. Other maps tell us how people live. Are they farmers or do they work in factories? We can use maps to learn many different things.

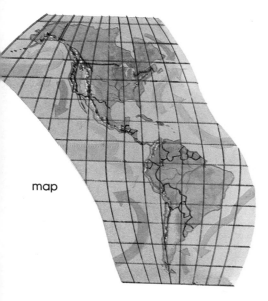
map

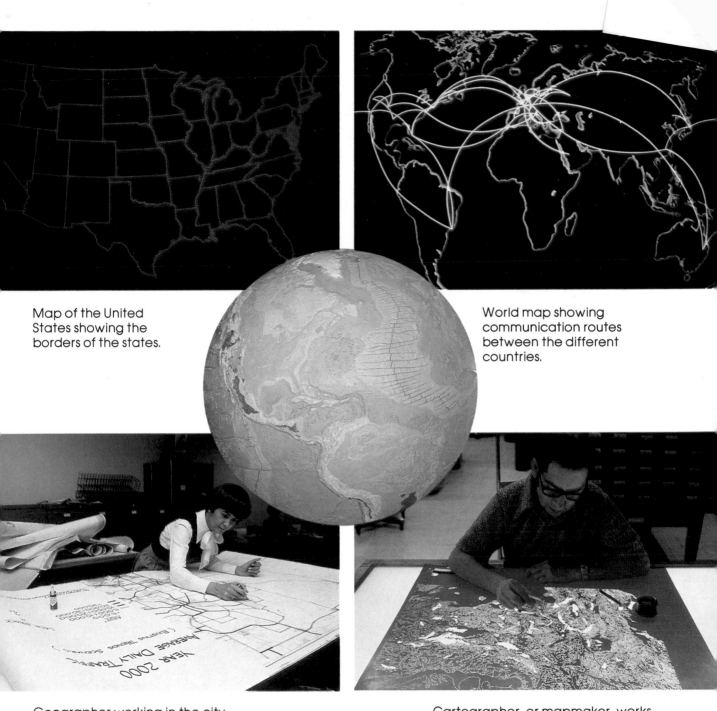

Map of the United States showing the borders of the states.

World map showing communication routes between the different countries.

Geographer working in the city planning department maps out transportation routes.

Cartographer, or mapmaker, works on a map showing the location of defense installations.

Soil samples (left) and water samples (right) are collected in the field for examination by experts in laboratories.

Not all geographers make maps. Some study the natural resources. They show us the location of natural resources, like oil, natural gas, and coal. Many of our resources will not last forever, we must use them wisely. Geographers help us do that.

oil

natural gas

coal

10

Geographers work with other scientists to learn about the earth. They study the reports written by scientists in the laboratory (above), geologists looking for minerals (right), and ecologists taking water samples in the Arctic (below).

A farm in Pennsylvania plants crops in strips to prevent soil erosion.

Some geographers teach people how to use their land properly. To do this, geographers study science. They learn all about soils, plants, and animals.

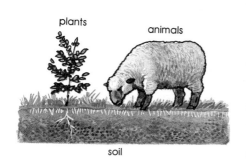

plants

animals

soil

Learning about soils and plants is very important. A geographer knows which plants will grow best in a particular soil. They know which kinds of animals can live best

13

Range erosion
studies provide
important
information.

in certain places.

Soil must also be
protected from poor
farming methods. Cutting
down the trees and
plants that protect soil
can cause erosion. The

soil erosion—wasteland

soil becomes dry and
loose and blows away.
When this happens, good
farmland is turned into
wasteland. Advice from a
geographer could have
helped save the land.

In this region of
Africa, cattle
must be watered
at wells. Years of
drought have
robbed the land
of its rich topsoil.

15

In cold climates people wear layers of protective clothing.

climate

Learning about climates is also very important for geographers. Climate affects the way people live. Eskimos live in a cold, dry climate. Amazon River Indians live in a hot, humid rain forest. Their lives are very different.

Where people live often

rain forest

In warmer climates the people wear lightweight clothes.

determines how they live. In many parts of the world, people who live near the ocean depend on fishing. People who live on mountains or in deserts often become animal herders. People who live where there is rich soil often become farmers. Geographers make maps that show how and where different people live.

The land often determines how people make their living. Shepherds need grasses for their sheep (top). Fishermen (above) need to live near water. Farmers (right) need good soil, rain, and sunshine to grow crops.

Field studies are important. The temperature samples taken in Kosciusko National Park (left) and measurements recording the rate of water flow in the stream (right) will be studied by geographers.

field study

A geographer uses actual field studies to learn about the earth. Maps of the earth's structure and soil maps

are made after studies
are done. Maps of ocean
currents and weather
patterns are made from
field studies and reports.

weather patterns

This computer-generated map of a weather system
and the photograph of Hurricane Gloria (inset)
were developed from photographs sent to earth
by satellites.

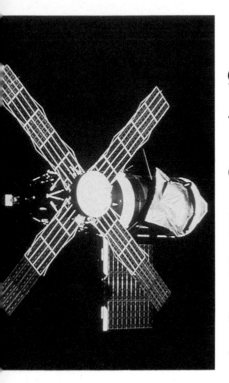

Skylab satellite

satellite

Today, some geographers use satellites to learn more about the earth. The satellites photograph the earth's landmasses and oceans at different times of year. These photographs show such details as schools of fish, diseased crops, and environmental pollution. Satellites send this valuable information back to earth.

A *Challenger* space shuttle photograph of the Washington, D. C., area (left) and a *Skylab* photograph of Great Britain (above) provided geographers with valuable information. Aerial photographs (below) are used to determine the damage boll weevils have done to farmland in Texas.

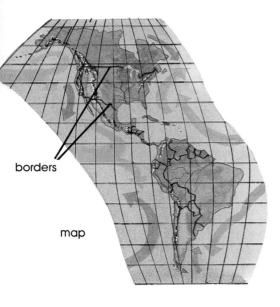

borders

map

Today, the need for knowledge of geography is as great as ever. More and more people are becoming world travelers. As world politics change, national borders and boundaries change with them. Even the names may change. As a result, maps are always changing too. It is the job of the geographer to keep the world informed.

A professor of geography (left) addresses his class at King Saud University. Third graders study the globe with their teacher.

Would you like to be a geographer? Geographers can do many different jobs. Some become teachers or work as researchers at universities.

Government maps must be accurate and up-to-date.

Others work for the government. They watch over land use, shifting populations, and natural resources. Geographers help the government plan for the future.

Geographers are also

City planners use maps when selecting the best places to build new parks.

needed in city planning. They help select routes for highways and sites for shopping centers. How we use our available land is important. Geographers help us make the right decisions.

The Portage Glacier in Alaska (left) and the game preserve in Loangue Valley National Park in Angola (right) attract tourists from all over the world.

The travel industry hires people with knowledge of geography as travel agents or guides. Businesses often hire geographers to learn more about the people and natural resources in

28

Tourists visit the Piazza Navona in Rome, Italy, and the Himalaya Mountains of Nepal.

other countries. That makes doing business much easier.

If you wonder about faraway places and want to learn more about the world, perhaps geography is for you!

WORDS YOU SHOULD KNOW

boundary(BOUND • ree) — an imaginary line where one country ends and another begins

climate(KLY • mit) — the usual weather conditions in a certain area

coal(KOLE) — a hard, black substance that burns and gives off heat

continent(KAHN • tih • nent) — one of the seven large masses of land on the earth

current(KER • int) — a moving stream of water within an ocean, often warmer or colder than the surrounding water

desert(DEZ • ert) — a dry, sandy area with very little rainfall, and few plants and animals

erosion(ih • ROH • jun) — the wearing away of rock and soil by the action of wind or water

Eskimos(ESS • kih • moze) — people who live in the very cold northern regions of the earth

factories(FAK • ter • eez) — buildings where such products as automobiles, chemicals, and furniture are made

herder(HER • der) — a person who tends herds of animals such as sheep or goats that are raised for meat or milk or wool

natural gas(NATCH • ril   GASS) — a gas that is formed in the earth and that can be burned as fuel

natural resources(NATCH • ril   REE • sore • siz) — supplies of materials found in the earth, such as iron and timber, that are used to make things

ocean(OH • shin) — the great body of salty water that covers much of the earth

oil(OYL) — a black liquid that is found in the earth and that can be made into gasoline and other fuels

researcher(REE • serch • er) — a person who does experiments to find new ways to make products or to learn more about science

satellite(SAT • ill • ite) — an artificial object that orbits the earth; some satellites relay TV pictures or take photographs of the earth

school(SKOOL) — a large group of fish that swim together

soil(SOYL) — the top layer of the earth's surface, where plants grow

INDEX

PHOTO CREDITS

© Cameramann International, Ltd.—4 (top left), 9 (bottom left, bottom right), 21, 26, 27
Journalism Services—10 (both photos), 12, 13, 14, 21 (left), 23 (bottom)
Norma Morrison—1
NASA—22
Root Resources—19 (top)
Tom Stack and Associates—6, 7 (right), 9 (top left, top right), 25 (left)
TSW, Click/Chicago Ltd.—7 (left), 11 (bottom), 20 (both photos), 23 (top left, top right), 28 (right)
Third Coast Stock Source—Cover, 25 (right)
Valan Photos—4 (top right, bottom), 9 (center), 11 (top left, top right), 15, 16, 17, 19 (bottom left, bottom right), 28 (left), 29 (both photos)

About the Author

Paul P. Sipiera is a professor of earth sciences at William Rainey Harper College in Palatine, Illinois. His principal areas of research are in the study of meteorites and volcanic rocks. He has participated in the United States Antarctic Research Program and is a member of The Explorers Club. When he is not studying science, he can be found traveling the world or working on his farm in Galena, Illinois.